CHILDREN'S ACTIVITY BOOK
MY HEART SAYS YES
BY KAMIONE CHAMBERS

ILLUSTRATED BY XANDER NESBITT

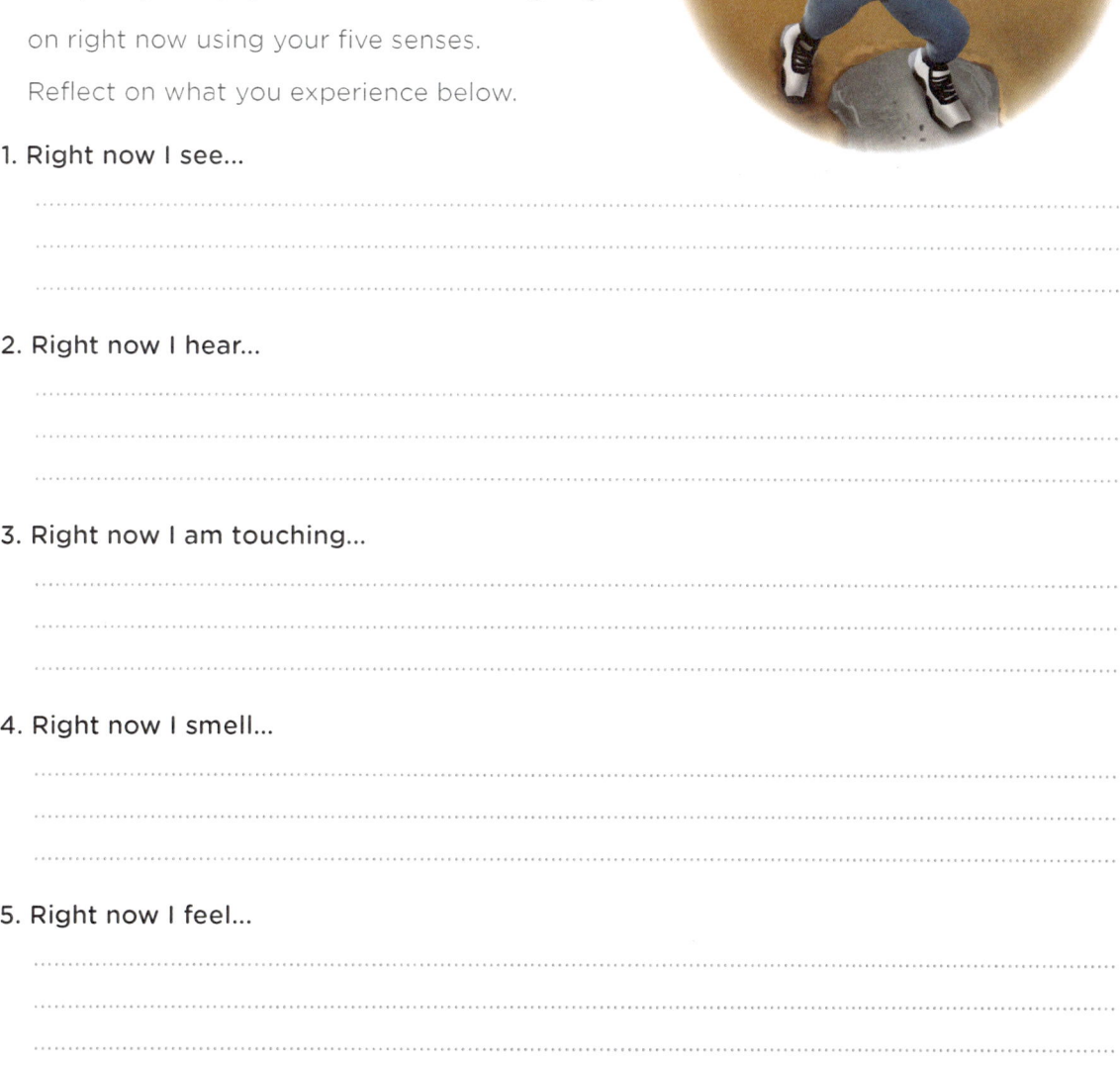

mindfulness series

THE PRESENT MOMENT

What does it mean to be present?

The word "present" can mean a gift, and it also describes what is happening right now, in the moment.

Sit quietly and pay attention to what is going on right now using your five senses.

Reflect on what you experience below.

1. Right now I see...

....

....

....

2. Right now I hear...

....

....

....

3. Right now I am touching...

....

....

....

4. Right now I smell...

....

....

....

5. Right now I feel...

....

....

....

mindfulness series

THE PRESENT MOMENT

What is the difference between the past, the present, and the future?

Below, write and/or draw about something that took place in the past, something that might take place in the future, and something that is happening right now.

Past: ....

Present: ....

Future: ....

HOW MANY CACTUS TREES STAND IN MONTEIL'S WAY?

PRACTICE COUNTING BACKWARDS

Help Monteil run across the track by writing down the missing numbers in backwards order on each of jungle roads below

Runway 1:

18		16		14	

Runway 2:

31			28	27	

Runway 3:

15				11	

Runway 4:

28					

Runway 5:

37					32

Runway 6:

50					

HOW MANY OF THE PROBLEMS CAN YOU SOLVE IN 1 MINUTE?

3 + 5	1 + 4	7 + 7	8 + 3	4 + 5	9 + 0
4 + 2	7 + 5	0 + 6	3 + 6	5 + 5	2 + 7
9 + 1	4 + 4	8 + 5	2 + 2	6 + 7	4 + 3
6 + 6	3 + 7	8 + 9	1 + 5	3 + 2	7 + 8
5 + 0	6 + 2	7 + 9	4 + 0	3 + 3	8 + 4
2 + 5	9 + 9	6 + 4	0 + 3	7 + 5	8 + 0
		0 + 0	4 + 9	8 + 8	3 + 2
		7 + 4	9 + 2	6 + 6	2 + 2
		1 + 1	1 + 6	9 + 3	5 + 6

HARRY SAYS CONNECT
THE DOTS AND SMILE

9

COMPLETE THE MAZE TO GIVE MONTEIL ENERGY WITH FRUITS AND VEGETABLES!

WORD SEARCH

```
Y  D  N  F  S  A  Y  E  Y  U  I  E  R  N
F  C  F  O  B  T  L  B  X  Y  U  J  L  J
G  D  S  I  Q  B  R  N  P  G  B  Z  E  C
S  Z  M  W  S  O  Z  O  Y  H  S  Y  A  L
K  X  A  O  U  O  F  Z  N  F  M  U  D  H
I  W  R  H  V  Z  M  E  H  G  A  S  E  V
H  J  T  M  X  H  M  P  A  Z  L  I  R  P
O  A  S  L  P  H  E  E  U  Z  U  O  T  A
Q  J  H  B  I  L  M  A  B  R  F  N  Y  H
K  D  X  W  O  R  O  W  R  X  P  K  R  W
A  M  K  A  B  U  B  Y  U  T  V  O  D  A
D  V  P  E  M  Q  S  N  R  J  Y  J  S  Y
B  X  F  O  Q  B  R  A  V  E  W  Y  C  E
M  T  L  F  U  S  X  Z  C  M  I  R  V  P
Z  O  C  O  R  Q  Z  U  O  X  N  G  B  A
```

purpose   leader   strong   faith

heart   smart   brave   win

11

LEARNING TO TELL TIME

Write the time under the first set of clocks. The first one has been done for you.

9:15

Now draw the hands on these analog clock faces to match the digital time already given.

The first one has been done for you.

9:45   12:15   3:30   7:00

10:15   6:00   5:15   11:00

PRACTICE COUNTING BACKWARDS

Help Monteil run across the track by writing down the missing

numbers in backwards order on each of jungle roads below

Runway 1:

18	17	16	15	14	13

Runway 2:

31	30	29	28	27	26

Runway 3:

15	14	13	12	11	10

Runway 4:

28	27	26	25	24	23

Runway 5:

37	36	35	34	33	32

Runway 6:

50	49	48	47	46	45

HOW MANY OF THE PROBLEMS CAN YOU SOLVE IN 1 MINUTE?

Answer Key

3 + 5 **8**	1 + 4 **5**	7 + 7 **14**	8 + 3 **11**	4 + 5 **9**	9 + 0 **9**
4 + 2 **6**	7 + 5 **12**	0 + 6 **6**	3 + 6 **9**	5 + 5 **10**	2 + 7 **9**
9 + 1 **10**	4 + 4 **8**	8 + 5 **13**	2 + 2 **4**	6 + 7 **13**	4 + 3 **7**
6 + 6 **12**	3 + 7 **10**	8 + 9 **17**	1 + 5 **6**	3 + 2 **5**	7 + 8 **15**
5 + 0 **5**	6 + 2 **8**	7 + 9 **16**	4 + 0 **4**	3 + 3 **6**	8 + 4 **12**
2 + 5 **7**	9 + 9 **18**	6 + 4 **10**	0 + 3 **3**	7 + 5 **12**	8 + 0 **8**
		0 + 0 **0**	4 + 9 **13**	8 + 8 **16**	3 + 2 **5**
		7 + 4 **11**	9 + 2 **11**	6 + 6 **12**	2 + 2 **4**
		1 + 1 **2**	1 + 6 **7**	9 + 3 **12**	5 + 6 **11**

14

COMPLETE THE MAZE TO GIVE MONTEIL ENERGY WITH FRUITS AND VEGETABLES!

Answer Key

WORD SEARCH

Answer Key

```
Y  D  N  F  S  A  Y  E  Y  U  I  E  R  N
F  C  F  O  B  T  L  B  X  Y  U  J  L  J
G  D  S  I  Q  B  R  N  P  G  B  Z  E  C
S  Z  M  W  S  O  Z  O  Y  H  S  Y  A  L
K  X  A  O  U  O  F  Z  N  F  M  U  D  H
I  W  R  H  V  Z  M  E  H  G  A  S  E  V
H  J  T  M  X  H  M  P  A  Z  L  I  R  P
O  A  S  L  P  H  E  E  U  Z  U  O  T  A
Q  J  H  B  I  L  M  A  B  R  F  N  Y  H
K  D  X  W  O  R  O  W  R  X  M  K  R  W
A  M  K  A  B  U  B  Y  U  T  V  O  D  A
D  V  P  E  M  Q  S  N  R  J  Y  J  S  Y
B  X  F  O  Q  B  R  A  V  E  W  Y  C  E
M  T  L  F  U  S  X  Z  C  M  I  R  V  P
Z  O  C  O  R  Q  Z  U  O  X  N  G  B  A
```

purpose   leader   strong   faith

heart   smart   brave   win

16

LEARNING TO TELL TIME

Write the time under the first set of clocks. The first one has been done for you.

9:15   4:00   8:30   12:45

2:00   10:45   7:15   1:30

Now draw the hands on these analog clock faces to match the digital time already given.

The first one has been done for you.

9:45   12:15   3:30   7:00

10:15   6:00   5:15   11:00

THINGS I'M THANKFUL FOR...